When Bad Things Happen

A Guide to Help Kids Cope

Written by
Ted O'Neal

Illustrated by
R. W. Alley

ONE
CARING
PLACE

Abbey Press
St. Meinrad, IN 47577

D1300612

To "Neal, Neal, Orange Peel,"
with love and laughter.

Text © 2003 Ted O'Neal
Illustrations © 2003 St. Meinrad Archabbey
Published by One Caring Place
Abbey Press
St. Meinrad, Indiana 47577

Library of Congress Catalog Number
2002117168

ISBN 0-87029-371-0

Printed in the United States of America

A Message to Parents, Teachers, and Other Caring Adults

As parents, teachers, *guardians* of our children, we try to *guard* them from life's many evils. And yet we can't—and we mustn't—shelter our children completely from all hurt. What we can and must do instead is be protectors, healers, and teachers of our children to the best of our abilities...in good times and in bad.

Keeping children from serious injury, neglect, and danger is a major responsibility for parents and teachers. Of course, it is also true that little children can learn big lessons from life's smaller tumbles and fumbles. As we adults know, some things must be learned the hard way or they are not learned at all. If a child were sheltered from every danger or pain, for instance, he or she would never get needed immunizations; or venture out into the cold snow to play and have fun; or face a demanding teacher or coach and learn about coping, working hard, and meeting goals.

Beyond all this, truly bad things *do* happen in life. Children can be hurt, confused, and sometimes seriously challenged by life's big hurts: the death of a dear one, an accident or an illness, the separation of one's parents, natural disasters, neighborhood crimes.

This coping guide for kids aims at helping them with these bigger hurts. The series of short, illustrated sections first present the child with a basic understanding of life's good and bad and in-betweens. The book then introduces a wide range of positive coping skills and responses to various hurts and harms of life.

In the end, the reader will learn helpful ways of responding to personal injuries and insults, as well as how to be a more understanding, adaptable, and caring person, no matter the circumstances.

"Life is good" is the major lesson of these pages. It is good, despite bad things that happen, because we human beings can learn—even when we are very small—how to cope, how to love, how to grow.

—Ted O'Neal

Good Times, Bad Times

Not everything goes right in the world, does it? Sometimes things go so wrong that even the big people who care about us can't seem to "fix" them.

Maybe one of your favorite toys gets broken, or your report card has some grades that are not so great. Maybe you get sick or hurt—or your mom or dad or grandparent does.

Sunshine is part of life—and so are thunderstorms. There are good times and there are bad times. And the bad times may not even be anybody's fault.

However You Feel Is Okay

When something very bad happens, you might want to cry or yell or run away and hide. You might have stomachaches or nightmares. You might feel:

confused   scared
tired   sick
bored   guilty
angry   lonely
sad   ashamed
worried

All these feelings are normal. You don't need to be ashamed or afraid of them. Talk about your feelings with someone close to you.

"Why?"

It's hard to understand why Grandma got sick, or why you have to move far away from friends. Ask your mom or dad to help you understand.

Even if you know the reasons, you don't have to like what happened. You can understand that your cat was hit by a car, but you will still feel mad and sad.

You might think you *made* a bad thing happen. If it rains on the day your dad takes you to a ballgame, you may feel like you are being punished somehow.

But rain just happens, and so do some bad things. There isn't any good reason. It isn't anybody's fault. You didn't cause it by being bad, and you can't undo it by being good.

Help Yourself

Don't let your worry, anger, or sadness be a secret. Even if grown-ups seem too busy to listen, make sure they know how you feel. You might be surprised to find out that they feel the same as you.

Some of your questions might upset people, because they aren't sure how to answer them. And some grown-ups—no matter how much they care about you—just don't know how to talk about bad things.

It's still good to find out how people are feeling and thinking—even if they are confused. It's good to know that you are not the only one feeling bad. It's good to know that you are safe and loved and will always be cared for.

Help Others

Each of us has special gifts to help us bring kindness to the world. When bad things happen, the world needs LOTS of kindness!

Can you write a letter to someone who is sad or sick or worried? Could you visit and talk with him or her?

Do you remember the nursery rhyme about "Humpty Dumpty"? He "had a great fall"—and "all the king's horses and all the king's men couldn't put Humpty together again."

You may not be able to put things "together again" either. But do what you can to help, even if it's something very small. Just trying will make you feel better.

God's Plan

Why does God let bad things happen? Not even the wisest people in the world know the answer to this question.

We believe God has a big plan for the whole universe, even though we do not understand it. We know God loves us and cares for us.

Like a Real Friend, God is always with us, no matter what happens. God sees all of our troubles and wants to help us. When we pray, we can tell God our true thoughts and feelings. We trust God will hear us and help us. We know God sometimes helps us through the hands and hugs of other people.

Being Brave

Being brave does not mean you are not afraid. Being brave means you are afraid—but you still do what you need to do.

If your grandma is very sick, it might be hard for you to keep your mind on your school work. But that is what you need to do. That is how you can be brave. Even just telling people you are afraid is a strong thing to do.

Sometimes you might wish you could be brave like your mom or dad or an army general. Even grown-ups get scared, though—just like you.

Truly brave people are smart people. They know that good is stronger than bad. Love is stronger than hate. We are all stronger than we think we are.

Be Yourself

When bad things happen, it seems like everything changes. But you are still you.

You can still do what you like to do. You can still play with your favorite games and friends. You can still read a book that you love, or treat yourself to your favorite dessert.

Even if things are not just like they were before, they can still be good. Enjoy and be thankful for all the things that are good in your life.

Do Something New

It's good to try new and different things, too. This will help to take your mind off your troubles for a while.

Maybe you could go to a new park or playground. If you live near a woods, you could take a hike with someone older. Try to spot some woodland creatures. Notice the trees and flowers and rocks in the creek.

It's a beautiful, wonderful world we live in, after all!

Remember the Heroes

There are many famous people—inventors, presidents, scientists—who had bad things happen to them. Yet they still did much good in the world. Abraham Lincoln was very poor as a child. Helen Keller was blind and deaf her whole life.

The people we call "heroes" know that life is hard sometimes, but bad times do not last forever. They know that people need to help each other, work together, and never give up.

Ordinary people can be heroes, too—when they are strong, loving, and forgiving. Are some of the people around you heroes?

Try to Forgive

Forgiving doesn't mean that we *like* what happened—or that we will *forget* it. Forgiving means we try to understand and let go of hurt and anger.

Forgiving isn't easy. If someone hits you on the playground for no reason, it's hard to forgive. But if no one ever forgave, then everyone would be hitting each other back all the time. And the hitting would go on and on.

If you are mad at your parents for letting something bad happen, talk to them about it. If you are mad at God, talk about it when you pray. God will listen and understand.

Do Good

The best thing to do about *bad* things is to do *good* things.

Lots of good can come from showing *faith*, *hope*, and *love*. Faith means believing in a God who loves us and wants the best for us. Hope means trusting that life will get better. Love means treating others kindly, the way we would like to be treated.

The best thing to do when something bad happens is to pour more good into the world. Practice faith, hope, and love!

Really Bad Things

Sometimes we hear about really bad things in the world—like crashes, fires, floods, or war.

If you are worried that something like this will happen to you, tell your parents or teacher. You can talk with them about all the things you do every day to stay safe and well.

When you go to bed at night, pray for the people who have to go through very bad things. Pray that everyone has a home and enough food. Pray that people are able to forgive each other and get along, so there will be no more war.

Life Changes

Lots of things in life can change—but some things never do. God will always love you. Your family will always love you. They will always take care of you.

Maybe you feel like *you* have changed. You might feel braver or more grown up. Maybe you have noticed your family or friends being more caring and loving than ever. Maybe you feel more loving, too.

And love is what our world needs all the time—when things are good, when things are bad, and when things are in-between.

Ted O'Neal is a husband, father, and writer living in southern Indiana. He is the author, with his daughter, Jenny, of the popular Elf-help Book for Kids *Respect: Dare to Care, Share, and Be Fair!* He has also written the adult Elf-help books *Nature Therapy* and *Garden Therapy*.

R. W. Alley is the illustrator for the popular Abbey Press adult series of Elf-help books, as well as an illustrator and writer of children's books. He lives in Barrington, Rhode Island, with his wife, daughter, and son.